Explore Space Probes

Lola Schaefer

Lerner Publications • Minneapolis

Lerner Publications Company
An imprint of Lerner Publishing Group, Inc.
241 First Avenue North
Minneapolis, MN 55401 USA

For reading levels and more information, look up this title at www.lernerbooks.com.

Main body text set in Billy Infant Regular. Typeface provided by SparkType.

Library of Congress Cataloging-in-Publication Data

Names: Schaefer, Lola M., 1950- author.
Title: Explore space probes / Lola Schaefer.
Description: Minneapolis, MN: Lerner Publications, [2023] | Series: Lightning bolt books.
    Exploring space | Includes bibliographical references and index. | Audience: Ages 6-9 |
    Audience: Grades 2-3 | Summary: "How do we know if there is water on Mars? We send
    probes to look around! Readers learn how scientists use space probes to study planets in
    our solar system . . . and beyond"—Provided by publisher.
Identifiers: LCCN 2021045421 (print) | LCCN 2021045422 (ebook) | ISBN 9781728457826
    (library binding) | ISBN 9781728463490 (paperback) | ISBN 9781728461595 (ebook)
Subjects: LCSH: Space probes—Juvenile literature. | Outer space—Exploration—Juvenile
    literature.
Classification: LCC TL795.3 .S33 2023 (print) | LCC TL795.3 (ebook) | DDC 629.43/5—dc23/
    eng/20211104

LC record available at https://lccn.loc.gov/2021045421
LC ebook record available at https://lccn.loc.gov/2021045422

Manufactured in the United States of America
1-50810-50149-3/22/2022

Table of Contents

Soil from Mars

The Mars rover Perseverance is a space probe. It traveled through space to study Mars.

It drills into the land for a soil sample. It moves on to find new samples.

Perseverance collects soil samples and places them where later missions can find them.

The Story of Space Probes

Space probes are uncrewed machines that explore space. They gather information and send it to Earth.

Some space probes land on moons or planets. Other space probes fly next to planets and take photos of them.

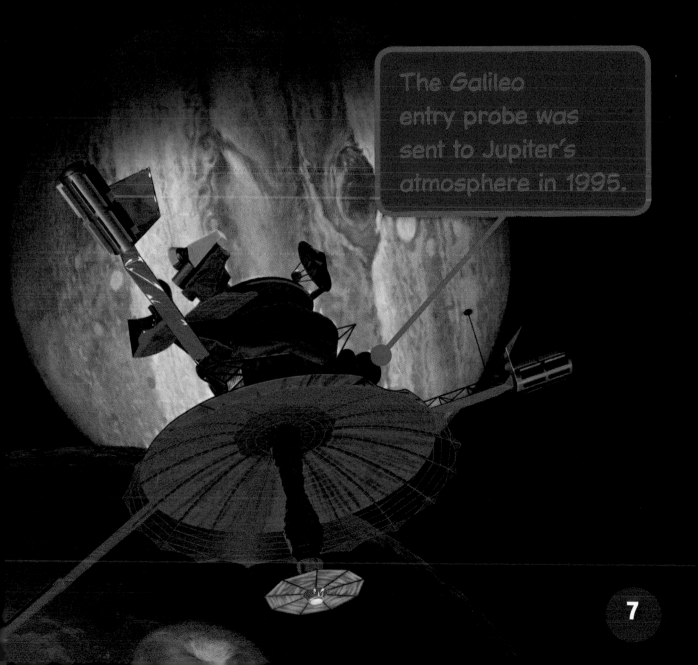

The *Galileo* entry probe was sent to Jupiter's atmosphere in 1995.

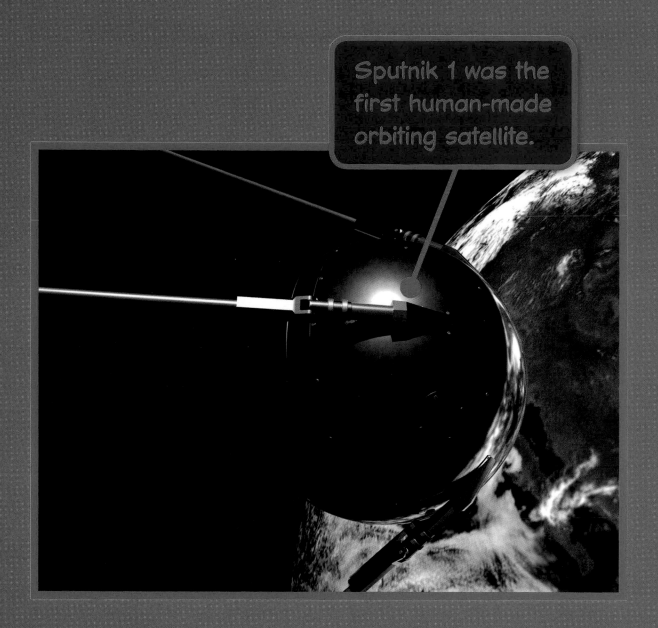

Sputnik 1 was the first human-made orbiting satellite.

The first space probes were called orbiters. They flew around Earth for only a few weeks.

Modern orbiters stay in space for a long time. They take photos and videos of objects in space.

The Mars Reconnaissance Orbiter orbits the planet to find and study water on Mars.

Landers are space probes that land on planets or moons. They take close-up photos. Sometimes they take samples of soils and gases.

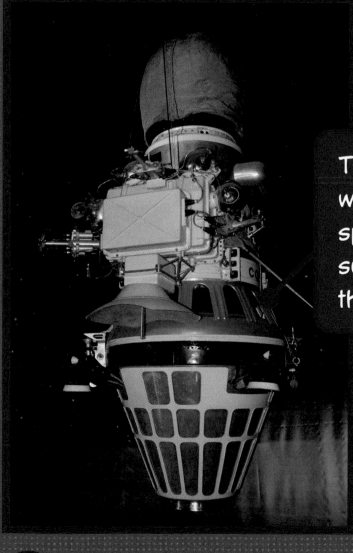

The Luna 9 lander was the first spacecraft to successfully land on the moon.

On its way to Saturn, the Cassini spacecraft flew past Jupiter and sent data and images back to Earth.

Space probes that fly next to different objects in space are called flyby probes. They take photos from space but do not land.

Space Probes in Action

Rockets launch probes into space. The probes transmit information to Earth with an antenna.

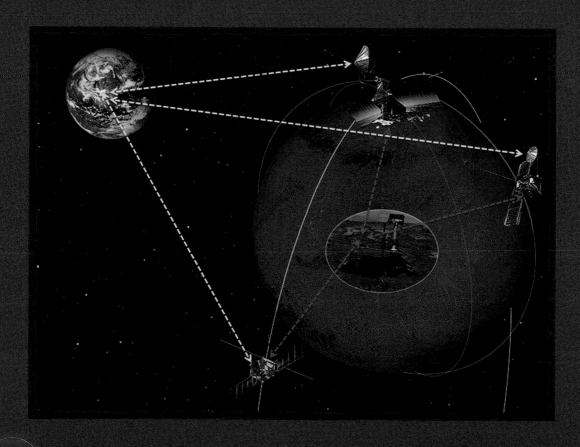

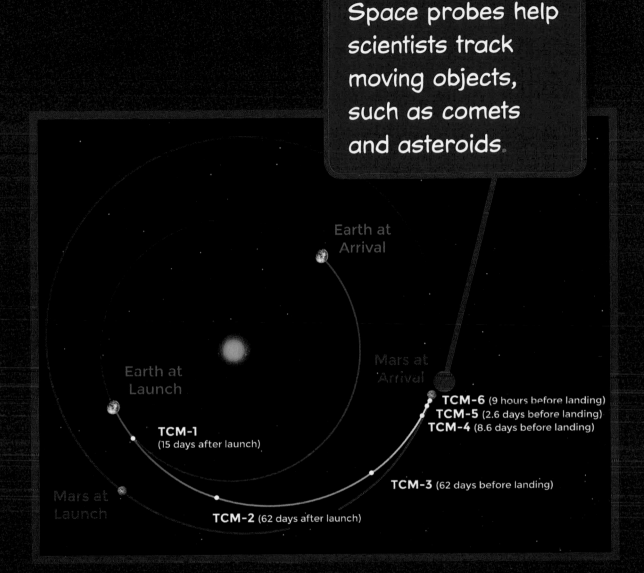

Space probes help scientists track moving objects, such as comets and asteroids.

Space probes send data day and night. This data helps scientists know more about objects in space.

Radio antennas around Earth track the space probes and receive their information. Sensors gather data about gases, heat, and the surfaces of planets, moons, and asteroids.

Scientists who study space use the data from space probes to learn more about the universe.

This data is shared with scientists all over the world. They work together to understand space and the objects in it.

Into the unknown

The data from space probes helps scientists make better probes. Landers will move over rocky surfaces more easily.

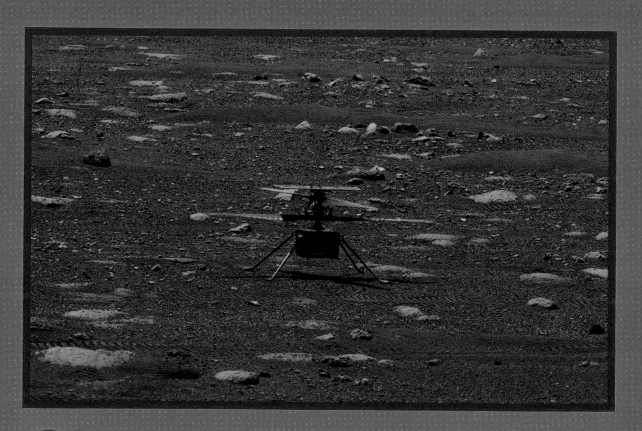

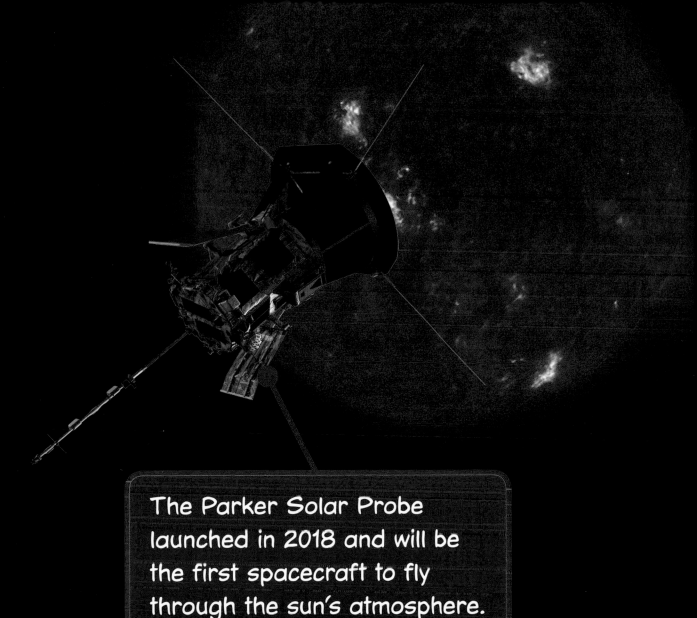

The Parker Solar Probe launched in 2018 and will be the first spacecraft to fly through the sun's atmosphere.

Flyby probes will travel farther in space. Cameras on orbiters will send us clearer photos of planets.

Future probes will get even closer to asteroids and the sun. Orbiters and landers will look for life on other planets.

Perseverance and other space probes are looking for signs of life on Mars.

If you want to know more about space, read about what space probes find. One day, you may make a space probe that will explore new worlds!

Space Probe Diagram

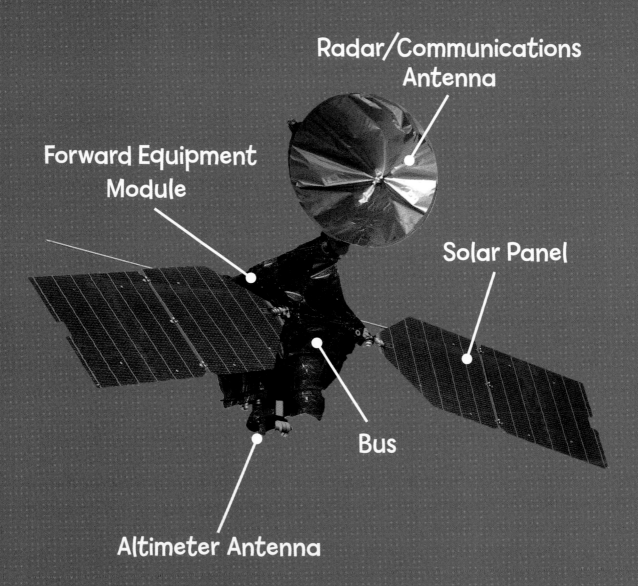

Radar/Communications Antenna

Forward Equipment Module

Solar Panel

Bus

Altimeter Antenna

Voyager 2 Flyby Spacecraft

On August 20, 1977, Voyager 2 entered space. It flew by Jupiter, Saturn, Uranus, and Neptune. On its path, it discovered new moons, planet rings, and even a giant dark spot on Neptune. It has left our solar system and is in interstellar space. Voyager 2 still transmits data to Earth so we can learn more about deep space.

Glossary

data: information or facts

launch: to send a rocket up into space

orbiter: a vehicle or device that travels around a planet or moon in space

sample: a small amount of something that shows what the rest of it is like

sensor: an instrument that can detect changes in heat, light, and sound and sends the information to a receiving device

surface: the outside or outermost layer of something

transmit: to send or pass something from one place to another

Learn More

Kiddle: Space Probe Facts for Kids
https://kids.kiddle.co/Space_probe

NASA: Curiosity Celebrates Another Year on Mars
https://www.nasa.gov/image-feature/curiosity
-celebrates-another-year-on-mars

National Geographic Kids: History of Space Travel
https://kids.nationalgeographic.com/space
/article/history-of-space-travel

Schaefer, Lola. *Explore Satellites*. Minneapolis:
Lerner Publications, 2023.

Statum, Hilary. *Solar System for Kids: A Junior
Scientist's Guide to Planets, Dwarf Planets,
and Everything Circling Our Sun*. Emeryville, CA:
Rockridge, 2020.

Woolf, Alex. *The Science of Spacecraft: The Cosmic
Truth about Rockets, Satellites, and Probes*. New
York: Franklin Watts, 2019.

Index

Photo Acknowledgments

Image credits: NASA/JPL-Caltech, pp. 4, 5, 13, 16; NASA/JPL, pp. 6, 9, 12, 20; NASA, p. 7; Rodichev Vitalii/Shutterstock.com, p. 8; Pline/Wikimedia Commons (CC BY-SA 3.0), p. 10; NASA/JPL-Caltech/SSI/CICLOPS/Kevin M. Gill/flickr (CC BY 2.0), p. 11; szc/E+/Getty Images, p. 14; NASA/Aubrey Gemignani, p. 15; NASA/Johns Hopkins APL/Steve Gribben/ Wikimedia Commons, p. 17; NASA/JPL/USGS, p. 18; NASA/Carla Cioffi, p. 19.

Cover: NASA.